Good Fast Food

Good Fast Food

Bounty
Books

First published in Great Britain in 2000 by
Hamlyn, a division of Octopus Publishing
Group Ltd

This edition published in 2008 by Bounty Books, a
division of Octopus Publishing Group Ltd
2–4 Heron Quays, London E14 4JP
Reprinted 2008 , 2009
An Hachette Livre UK Company

ISBN: 978-0-7537 16-56-4

A CIP catalogue record for this book is available
from the British Library

Printed and bound in China

Notes

1 Standard level spoon measurements are
used in all recipes.

1 tablespoon = one 15 ml spoon
1 teaspoon = one 5 ml spoon

2 Both imperial and metric measurements
have been given in all recipes. Use one set of
measurements only and not a mixture of both.

3 Measurements for canned foods have been
given as a standard metric equivalent.

4 Eggs should be medium unless otherwise
stated. The Department of Health advises that
eggs should not be consumed raw. This book
may contain dishes made with lightly cooked
eggs. It is prudent for more vulnerable people,
such as pregnant and nursing mothers,
invalids, the elderly, babies and young
children, to avoid uncooked or lightly cooked
dishes made with eggs. Once prepared, these
dishes should be used immediately.

5 Milk should be full fat unless otherwise
stated.

6 Poultry should always be cooked
thoroughly. To test if poultry is cooked, pierce
the flesh through the thickest part with a
skewer or fork – the juices should run clear,
never pink or red.

7 Fresh herbs should be used unless
otherwise stated. If unavailable, use dried
herbs as an alternative but halve the
quantities stated.

8 Pepper should be freshly ground black
pepper unless otherwise stated; season
according to taste.

9 Ovens should be preheated to the specified
temperature – if using a fan-assisted oven,
follow the manufacturer's instructions for
adjusting the time and the temperature.

10 Do not re-freeze a dish that has been
frozen previously.

11 This book includes dishes made with nuts
and nut derivatives. It is advisable for
customers with known allergic reactions to
nuts and nut derivatives and those who may be
potentially vulnerable to these allergies,
such as pregnant and nursing mothers,
invalids, the elderly, babies and young
children, to avoid dishes made with nuts and
nut oils. It is also prudent to check the labels
of pre-prepared ingredients for the possible
inclusion of nut derivatives.

12 Vegetarians should look for the 'V' symbol
on a cheese to ensure it is made with
vegetarian rennet. There are vegetarian forms
of Parmesan, feta, Cheddar, Cheshire, red
Leicester, dolcelatte and many goats' cheeses,
among others.

Whether you are looking for a starter for a dinner party or simply don't feel hungry enough for a proper meal, you'll find a mouthwatering choice here, including soups, salads and egg dishes and lots of clever new ways with vegetables.

Fish is at its best when cooked quickly or for just long enough to turn the flesh opaque. The recipes in this chapter range from all over the world, from oriental Rapid-fried Chilli Prawns and Mexican-inspired Red Snapper with Lime and Coriander, to a luxurious Sole Marsala with Parmesan Cheese from Italy and Salmon, Olive and Rocket Baguettine from France.

Chicken is probably the most versatile of all meats. Here, black olives, green peppers, peanut butter and port are among the flavoursome ingredients that speedily transform pieces of supermarket chicken into delicious meals. For a touch of variety, there are recipes for duck, turkey and chicken livers as well.

Delicious main courses, based on beef, lamb, pork and veal can all be put together in about 30 minutes, or even less. Whether you are looking for a special occasion treat, such as Green Peppercorn Steak, or a filling dish for a hungry family, like Sausage Frittata, you'll find the answer here.

Give your meals a happy ending with a quick but satisfying dessert, based on fresh fruit or luscious plain, dark chocolate, or enjoy a break for tea or coffee with delicious home-made cookies and muffins.

contents

introduction

Appetizing and nourishing meals put together in minutes are a basic requirement of modern life. After a busy day, most people simply don't have the time or the energy to spend long hours in the kitchen. This book has been compiled with this need in mind and most of the dishes can be made in 30 minutes or even less. Some require a minimum of attention a few hours ahead for tasks such as putting meat into a marinade, infusing spices and flavourings in olive oil to make a fragrant dressing, or chilling a dessert.

Oriental cooking and griddling are two styles of cooking to look to for inspiration when you want to prepare a quick meal. Far eastern taste is for food cooked crisply at high temperatures rather than the slow stews that are part of western cooking tradition. The eastern style is also for several small dishes served at the same time – rather than one large one – and the recipes in this book have been chosen with this in mind. If you wish to adapt them to western style, increase the quantities and serve them with plenty of rice or noodles.

Stir-frying

Stir-frying, a technique developed centuries ago in China, is a very speedy cooking method, but it does require top quality meat or a lengthy marinating time. A wok is an enormous bonus to anyone who needs to get meals together in a hurry. Its secret lies in its shape as the high sides and rounded bottom mean that the cook can stir and turn the food around over a high heat, so that it cooks evenly. The heat is conducted more quickly than in a conventionally shaped pan, so the ingredients cook in the minimum of time, retaining their natural colour and flavour.

The most useful sort of wok for stir-frying, and the cheapest, is the inexpensive Chinese one-handled wok, usually made of carbon steel, which is a good conductor of heat, and which can be bought at department stores and Asian supermarkets. Stir-frying is best done on a gas cooker as the heat is quickly adjustable and the design of the hob means that the wok is steady. This said, nonstick woks, although they are not such good conductors of heat, have the advantage that they require the minimum of fat and are easier to clean.

Because stir-frying is so quick, all the preparation must be completed first. Once you have started to cook, there will be no time to hunt for a missing ingredient or chop a vegetable. Chop all the ingredients into pieces of a uniform size and line them up by the hob with all the herbs and spices you will require. Use only the best quality ingredients as the food must cook in the shortest possible time. First preheat the wok over a low to moderate heat, then heat the oil. This is important because if the oil and the food are added to a cold wok they may stick. Food should start cooking as soon as it goes into the wok.

Griddling

The griddle pan, the most recent addition to the serious cook's kitchen equipment, looks like a frying pan but is much heavier and has a ridged surface. The modern development of the girdles and bakestones, used since time immemorial for baking breads, scones and cakes, it cooks on the principle of a dry, searing heat which seals food on the outside and locks in the flavours and juices. However, the heat should be lowered after the initial searing otherwise you may end up with food that is burned on the outside but raw inside. A crust should form on the bottom of the food before you turn it over otherwise it will stick to the pan. Since oil and butter are not needed, although griddle pans can be brushed with a little oil if you wish, griddling is very much in keeping with today's nutritional thinking, being an efficient low-fat cooking method suitable for meat, fish, poultry, vegetables and even fruits. Like stir-frying, because it is a speedy technique griddling also requires good quality ingredients.

'The world is so fast that there are days when the person who says it can't be done is interrupted by the person who is doing it.'

Anonymous

The Storecupboard

Cooking quick meals requires a certain amount of organization. Make sure that your storecupboard is regularly topped up with basics of all sorts including herbs and spices. If your taste is for Mediterranean food, good quality extra virgin olive oil, balsamic vinegar, pine nuts, sun-dried tomatoes, tomato purée, garlic, lemons, cans of tomatoes, cans of beans for salads and a selection of different types of pasta are essential. For oriental cooking, make sure you have bottles of dark and light soy sauce, Thai fish sauce, cans of coconut milk and blocks of creamed coconut, curry pastes, fresh root ginger and Chinese rice wine. Ready-made stocks from the supermarket are a good substitute for home-made stocks and can be stored in the freezer, while, also from the supermarket, vegetables, trimmed and sliced, bags of salad leaves and spinach, washed and ready to cook or to add to a dressing, all help to speed things up.

pesto dressing

Italian pesto sauce is addictive. Here it is made into a dressing which can be served with salads of all sorts.

25 g (1 oz) basil leaves

25 g (1 oz) Parmesan cheese, freshly grated

4 tablespoons white wine vinegar

1 tablespoon pine nuts

1 garlic clove, crushed

125 ml (4 fl oz) extra virgin olive oil

pepper

Combine the basil, Parmesan, vinegar, pine nuts and garlic in a food processor or blender with pepper to taste and purée to a fairly smooth paste. Drizzle in the olive oil through the feeder tube until the mixture becomes thick and smooth. Pour into a jug or bowl and use as required.

Serves 4

Preparation time: 5 minutes

tapenade

This black olive paste from Provence makes a lovely spread for toast and pizzas as well as a sauce to go with grilled fish. It can also be served with crudités or spread on cocktail biscuits. Use the juiciest olives you can find, for maximum flavour. If you have time to pit your own olives, you will need about twice the weight given here.

125 g (4 oz) pitted black olives

2 garlic cloves, chopped

25 g (1 oz) capers, drained and washed

2 canned anchovy fillets in oil, drained and chopped

1 tablespoon chopped parsley

1 teaspoon chopped thyme

pinch of mustard powder

2 tablespoons extra virgin olive oil

pepper

Place all the ingredients except the oil in a food processor or blender and purée to a fairly smooth paste. Transfer to a screw-top jar and stir in the oil. Tapenade can be stored in the refrigerator for up to 1 week.

Serves 4

Preparation time: 5 minutes

spinach & broccoli soup •

tuscan bean soup •

creamy corn & chicken chowder •

smoked mackerel & cream cheese pâté •

golden salad •

beetroot & orange salad •

ribbon vegetable stir-fry •

thai green bean salad •

roasted asparagus with coriander & lime •

potatoes wrapped in prosciutto •

tempura vegetables •

thai green curry with straw mushrooms •

aubergine, haloumi & cumin bruschetta •

grilled greek pitta pockets •

stuffed thai omelette •

savoury soufflé omelette •

three-cheese macaroni •

young spinach with cockles & mustard sauce •

starters
& snacks

2 tablespoons olive oil

50 g (2 oz) butter

1 onion, diced

1 garlic clove, crushed

2 potatoes, chopped

250 g (8 oz) broccoli, chopped

300 g (10 oz) spinach, washed and chopped

900 ml (1½ pints) chicken or vegetable stock

125 g (4 oz) Gorgonzola cheese, crumbled into small pieces

juice of ½ lemon

½ teaspoon grated nutmeg

salt and pepper

75 g (3 oz) toasted pine nuts, to garnish

crusty bread, to serve

1 Heat the oil and butter in a saucepan, add the onion and garlic and sauté for 3 minutes.

2 Add the chopped potatoes, broccoli, spinach and stock, bring to the boil and simmer for 15 minutes.

3 This soup can be puréed in a food processor or blender or left with chunky pieces. Add the Gorgonzola to the soup with the lemon juice, nutmeg and salt and pepper to taste. Garnish with the toasted pine nuts and serve with warm crusty bread.

Serves 4
Preparation time: 10 minutes
Cooking time: 20 minutes

spinach & broccoli soup

tuscan bean soup

1 Heat the oil in a saucepan, add the shallots, garlic, bacon, carrot, celery and red pepper and cook, stirring occasionally, for 5 minutes.

2 Add the beans, stock, bay leaf, oregano and marjoram, bring to the boil and simmer for 15 minutes, skimming off any scum that may come from the beans.

3 Taste and season well with salt and pepper, then add the chopped parsley. To serve, ladle the soup into warmed bowls and drizzle each one with a little olive oil.

2 tablespoons olive oil

4 shallots, chopped

2 garlic cloves, crushed

150 g (5 oz) piece of unsmoked bacon, diced

1 carrot, diced

2 celery sticks, diced

½ red pepper, cored, deseeded and diced

400 g (13 oz) can borlotti beans, drained and rinsed

1 litre (1¾ pints) chicken stock

1 bay leaf

1 teaspoon chopped oregano

1 teaspoon chopped marjoram

handful of flat leaf parsley, chopped

salt and pepper

extra virgin olive oil, to serve

Serves 4

Preparation time: 5 minutes

Cooking time: 25 minutes

creamy corn
& chicken chowder

1 Melt the butter or margarine in a large heavy-based saucepan. Add the onion, red pepper and potatoes and fry over a moderate heat for 5 minutes, stirring occasionally.

2 Sprinkle in the flour and cook over a gentle heat, stirring constantly, for 1 minute. Gradually stir in the stock and bring to the boil, stirring, then lower the heat, cover the pan and cook for 10 minutes.

3 Stir in the sweetcorn, chicken, milk, parsley and salt and pepper to taste, then replace the lid and simmer over a low heat for a further 10 minutes, until the potatoes are just tender. Taste and, if necessary, adjust the seasoning. Serve the chowder hot in warmed individual soup bowls, with plenty of crusty bread.

25 g (1 oz) butter or margarine

1 large onion, chopped

1 small red pepper, cored, deseeded and diced

625 g (1¼ lb) potatoes, diced

25 g (1 oz) plain flour

750 ml (1¼ pints) chicken stock

175 g (6 oz) frozen sweetcorn, defrosted

250 g (8 oz) cooked chicken, chopped

450 ml (¾ pint) milk

3 tablespoons chopped parsley

½ teaspoon salt

freshly ground white pepper

crusty bread, to serve

Serves 4–6

Preparation time: 5 minutes

Cooking time: 25 minutes

smoked mackerel & cream cheese pâté

1 Cream the butter and cheese together, then stir in the fish, lemon juice, chives and pepper to taste. Beat until the mixture is smooth.

2 Divide the pâté equally between 4 individual ramekins. Press a bay leaf on to the top of each dish to garnish. Wholemeal toast goes very well with this pâté.

■ Another attractive way to present this pâté is with a layer of melted butter poured over the top of each portion. Press a bay leaf into each ramekin before the butter sets. Cool, then cover with clingfilm. It can be stored in the refrigerator for up to 2 days.

75 g (3 oz) butter, softened

175 g (6 oz) full-fat soft cheese

375 g (12 oz) smoked mackerel fillets, skinned and flaked

2 teaspoons lemon juice

1 tablespoon snipped chives

pepper

4 small bay leaves, to garnish

wholemeal toast, to serve

Serves 4

Preparation time: 20 minutes

golden salad

1 Skin the mackerel fillets and slice each one into 4 pieces.

2 To make the orange dressing, mix together the orange rind and juice, tomato juice, cayenne pepper, honey and chives in a large bowl.

3 Toss the oranges, apples, celery and walnuts in the dressing, then carefully stir in the mackerel.

4 Line a serving platter with the endive or lettuce leaves, if using, and spoon the salad over them. Garnish with the orange slices.

4 smoked mackerel fillets

2 large oranges, peeled and divided into segments

2 dessert apples, cored and thinly sliced

2 young celery sticks, thinly sliced

2 tablespoons walnut halves

curly endive or lettuce leaves (optional)

4 thin orange slices, to garnish

Orange Dressing:

1 teaspoon grated orange rind

3 tablespoons orange juice

2 tablespoons tomato juice

large pinch of cayenne pepper

1 tablespoon clear honey

2 tablespoons finely snipped chives

Serves 4

Preparation time: 25 minutes

beetroot & orange salad

1 Peel the oranges, removing all the pith. Holding them over a bowl to catch the juice, divide them into segments. Remove the flesh from the membranes and cut the segments in half. Arrange the orange pieces in a serving dish, with the beetroot.

2 To make the dressing, add the vinegar, lemon juice, sugar, garlic, mustard powder and herbs to the bowl containing the orange juice. Whisk to mix, then gradually whisk in the oil. Taste the dressing and add salt and pepper as required. Pour the dressing over the salad, garnish with the watercress and serve.

3 oranges

375 g (12 oz) cooked beetroot, cut into matchsticks

1 tablespoon wine vinegar or cider vinegar

1 teaspoon lemon juice

pinch of sugar

1 small garlic clove, crushed

¼ teaspoon mustard powder

1 tablespoon chopped mixed herbs

3 tablespoons extra virgin olive oil

salt and pepper

watercress sprigs, to garnish

Serves 4

Preparation time: 20 minutes

ribbon vegetable stir-fry

1 Heat a wok until hot. Add the oil and heat over a moderate heat until hot but not smoking. Add the vegetables and garlic and stir-fry for 2 minutes. Add salt to taste and plenty of pepper. Serve immediately.

■ Peeling whole vegetables into ribbons makes an attractive and unusual form of presentation. Any kind of vegetable peeler can be used, but for speed, use a swivel-blade peeler.

2 tablespoons olive oil, walnut oil or vegetable oil

250 g (8 oz) carrots, peeled into ribbons

250 g (8 oz) courgettes, peeled into ribbons

1 green or red pepper, cored, deseeded and cut into matchsticks

2 garlic cloves, crushed

salt and pepper

Serves 4

Preparation time: 10 minutes

Cooking time: about 5 minutes

thai green bean salad

1 Cook the green beans in boiling water for 6 minutes, then drain well and set aside.

2 Put the coconut milk into a saucepan over a gentle heat, add the tofu and stir until partly melted. Remove the pan from the heat, add the beans and all the remaining ingredients. Stir thoroughly and turn out on to a serving dish. Serve the salad at room temperature.

■ To prepare crushed roasted nuts, dry-fry 25 g (1 oz) unroasted peanuts or cashew nuts in a frying pan, stirring constantly until they turn golden. Remove from the heat and leave to cool. Place the nuts in a plastic bag and break into small pieces with a rolling pin.

50 g (2 oz) thin green beans, thinly sliced

100 ml (3½ fl oz) coconut milk

100 g (3½ oz) soft tofu

1 shallot, sliced

25 g (1 oz) Crushed Roasted Nuts (see Cook's Tip below)

1 teaspoon crushed dried chillies

1 tablespoon lime juice

1 teaspoon sugar

2 tablespoons soy sauce

1 teaspoon salt

Serves 4
Preparation time: 10 minutes
Cooking time: 10 minutes

1 Trim the asparagus and use a potato peeler to peel about 5 cm (2 inches) off the base of each stalk. Arrange the asparagus in a single layer in a shallow roasting tin.

2 Spoon 4 tablespoons of the olive oil over the asparagus and shake lightly to mix. Roast in a preheated oven, 200°C (400°F), Gas Mark 6, for about 20 minutes, until just tender, turning the asparagus once during cooking. Leave to cool.

3 Transfer the roasted asparagus spears to a shallow dish and spoon the remaining olive oil and the lime juice over the top. Sprinkle with salt and pepper and toss lightly. Garnish with torn coriander leaves and lime wedges.

750 g (1½ lb) asparagus spears

8 tablespoons olive oil

3 tablespoons lime juice

coarse sea salt and pepper

To Garnish:

torn coriander leaves

lime wedges

Serves 4–6

Preparation time: 10 minutes, plus cooling

Cooking time: about 20 minutes

roasted asparagus with coriander & lime

potatoes wrapped in prosciutto

1 Wrap each potato in a slice of prosciutto.

2 Heat a griddle pan, add the wrapped potatoes and cook on all sides until the prosciutto is golden and crunchy. This will take about 8 minutes. Serve sprinkled with sea salt flakes and pepper.

12 new potatoes, boiled but unpeeled

12 long, thin slices of prosciutto

sea salt flakes and pepper

Serves 4
Preparation time: 15 minutes
Cooking time: 10 minutes

■ If you are feeding a lot of people, a good alternative to prosciutto is very thinly sliced bacon, which works well in this recipe and is less expensive.

tempura vegetables

1 First prepare the vegetables. Trim the broccoli and cauliflower into florets and blanch, then drain well. Peel the carrot and cut it into sticks. Trim and slice the mushrooms. Slice the onion into rings.

2 To make the batter, sift the flour and salt into a bowl. Beat in the eggs, then the warm water.

3 Heat the oil in a deep saucepan or wok. Quickly dip the prepared vegetables into the batter and then cook in the hot oil, in batches, for about 2 minutes, turning halfway through. Drain on kitchen paper and keep warm. Serve at once with a dipping sauce.

750 g (1½ lb) vegetables, such as a selection of broccoli, cauliflower, carrot, mushrooms, onion

oil, for deep-frying

Batter:

250 g (8 oz) plain flour

pinch of salt

2 eggs

250 ml (8 fl oz) warm water

Serves 12
Preparation time: 20 minutes
Cooking time: 10–12 minutes

■ Tempura is one of Japan's best-known dishes. Ready-made sauces suitable for dipping are soy sauce, oyster sauce, chilli sauce and mushroom sauce. Equal quantities of soy sauce and dry sherry stirred together also make a good dipping sauce.

thai green curry with straw mushrooms

1 Heat the coconut milk in a large saucepan with the curry paste, stirring until thoroughly blended.

2 Stir in the stock, then add the aubergines, sugar, salt, fish sauce or soy sauce, ginger and mushrooms. Bring to the boil and cook, stirring, for 2 minutes. Add the green pepper, lower the heat and cook for 1 minute.

3 Serve the curry in warmed bowls, garnished with the basil leaves and drizzled with coconut milk.

300 ml (½ pint) canned coconut milk

40 g (1½ oz) ready-made Thai green curry paste

300 ml (½ pint) vegetable stock

4 small round aubergines, each cut into 8 pieces

40 g (1½ oz) palm sugar or light muscovado sugar

1 teaspoon salt

4 teaspoons Thai fish sauce or soy sauce

25 g (1 oz) fresh root ginger, sliced

425 g (14 oz) can straw mushrooms, drained and rinsed

50 g (2 oz) green pepper, cut into matchstick strips

To Garnish:

handful of basil leaves

2 tablespoons coconut milk

Serves 4

Preparation time: 7 minutes

Cooking time: 10 minutes

aubergine, haloumi
& cumin bruschetta

1 Dry-fry the cumin seeds in a small frying pan until they start to pop and give off a smoky aroma. Add the oil and lemon rind, then remove the pan from the heat, cover and leave to infuse for several hours.

2 Heat a griddle pan and cook the aubergine slices for 4–5 minutes on each side. Remove the aubergines from the griddle and dip each slice into the cumin-scented oil, reserving the remaining oil. Spread the aubergine slices on a plate to cool to room temperature.

3 Just before serving, prepare the bruschetta. Heat the griddle pan, add the slices of bread and toast on each side. Add the haloumi and cook on each side for 1–2 minutes, turning it carefully with a palette knife or spatula. Rub the toast all over with the cut garlic halves and drizzle with olive oil. Toss the rocket leaves in the remaining cumin oil and heap onto the bruschetta. Arrange the slices of aubergine and haloumi on top and serve immediately.

1 tablespoon cumin seeds

4 tablespoons extra virgin olive oil, plus extra for drizzling

grated rind of 1 lemon

2 small aubergines, each cut lengthways into 4 slices

4 thick slices of day-old country bread

250 g (8 oz) haloumi cheese, cut into 4 slices

2 garlic cloves, halved

125 g (4 oz) rocket leaves

Serves 4

Preparation time: 5 minutes, plus infusing and cooling

Cooking time: 20–25 minutes

Haloumi is a semi-hard rather salty cheese from Cyprus, made from goats' milk. It has a slightly rubbery texture and griddles particularly well.

grilled greek
pitta pockets

1 Cut a slit across the top of each pitta bread but not through to the base. Gently open out the bread through the slit to form a pocket.

2 To make the filling, mix the lamb with the mushrooms, spring onions, lettuce, tomatoes, olives, dressing, and salt and pepper to taste. Blend well.

3 Stuff the pitta pockets equally with the filling and place on a grill rack. Sprinkle the cheese on top. Place under a preheated moderately hot grill and cook for 5–6 minutes, until the cheese has melted and is golden and bubbly. Serve at once.

4 pitta breads

75 g (3 oz) haloumi cheese, grated

Filling:

125 g (4 oz) cooked lamb, finely shredded

50 g (2 oz) mushrooms, thinly sliced

1 small bunch of spring onions, chopped

2 lettuce leaves, shredded

2 tomatoes, skinned, deseeded and chopped

8 black olives, pitted and sliced

2–3 tablespoons ready-made yogurt salad dressing

salt and pepper

Serves 4

Preparation time: 20 minutes

Cooking time: 5–6 minutes

1 Heat a wok, add 2 tablespoons of the oil and heat again. Add the garlic and stir-fry until just golden. Add the minced pork, fish sauce, sugar, onion and tomato and season with pepper. Stir-fry the pork and vegetable mixture for 5–10 minutes, until the pork is lightly browned and the onion is golden but not browned.

2 Heat the remaining oil in a clean wok, tilting it so that the oil coats the entire surface. Pour away and discard any excess oil. Add the beaten eggs, tilting the wok in all directions to form an omelette.

3 Put the stir-fried pork and vegetable mixture in the centre of the cooked omelette. Fold down the four sides like a parcel. Serve at once, folded side down, garnished with coriander sprigs and chilli flowers.

3 tablespoons vegetable oil

1 garlic clove, crushed

125 g (4 oz) minced pork

1 tablespoon Thai fish sauce

½ teaspoon sugar

125 g (4 oz) finely chopped onion

1 tomato, skinned and chopped

3 eggs, beaten

pepper

To Garnish:

coriander sprigs

2 red chillies, sliced stem to tip and opened out to look like flowers

Serves 2	
Preparation time: 10 minutes	
Cooking time: 12–17 minutes	

stuffed thai omelette

savoury soufflé omelette

1 Separate the eggs and beat the yolks with salt and pepper to taste, adding about ½ teaspoon of water. Heat the butter in a large, heavy-based frying pan.

2 Whisk the egg whites until they stand in peaks, then fold into the yolks just before cooking.

3 Pour the eggs into the pan and cook on the hob until just set on the bottom. Place the pan under a preheated moderate grill and cook until the omelette is set on top.

4 Cut the omelette lightly through the centre to make it easier to fold and add the filling of your choice. Fold away from the handle of the pan and tip on to a warmed plate.

■ This soufflé omelette can be made with a variety of fillings. Three are suggested above; others include 3 tablespoons flaked white or smoked fish in a Béchamel sauce or 3 tablespoons finely diced ham.

4 eggs

25–50 g (1–2 oz) butter

salt and pepper

Savoury Fillings:

Cheese:
3 tablespoons grated Cheddar cheese

Tomato:
2 plum tomatoes, skinned and chopped

2–3 basil leaves, chopped

Chicken:
3 tablespoons finely diced cooked chicken

Serves 2

Preparation time: 5 minutes, plus preparing the filling

Cooking time: 4–5 minutes

1 Place the water, salt and oil in a large saucepan and bring to the boil. Add the macaroni, keeping the water boiling. Reduce the heat slightly and cook for 8–10 minutes, or according to the packet instructions, stirring occasionally, until it is tender.

2 Drain the macaroni, rinse with hot water and drain again. Melt a little butter in a saucepan and, using 2 forks, toss the pasta evenly to coat.

3 To make the sauce, melt the butter or margarine in a saucepan, add the flour and stir constantly. When combined, add the milk, Worcestershire sauce, salt, pepper, chilli and mustard powder. Bring to the boil, stirring. Reduce the heat and cook gently for 2–3 minutes.

4 Stir the macaroni into the sauce until evenly coated. Mix together the three cheeses, reserving one-third for sprinkling. Add the remaining cheese to the sauce, mix well and pour into a buttered ovenproof dish. Sprinkle with the reserved cheese and the breadcrumbs. Place the dish under a preheated moderate grill and cook for about 5 minutes, until the top is golden brown. Serve immediately with slices of mixed peppers and garnished with parsley.

1.5 litres (2½ pints) water

1 teaspoon salt

1 tablespoon vegetable oil

250 g (8 oz) wholewheat macaroni

butter, to finish

parsley sprigs, to garnish

mixed peppers, sliced, to serve

Cheese Sauce:

50 g (2 oz) butter or margarine

50 g (2 oz) plain flour

750 ml (1¼ pints) milk

1 teaspoon Worcestershire sauce

¼ teaspoon salt

pinch of pepper

pinch of chilli powder

¼ teaspoon mustard powder

125 g (4 oz) Gruyère cheese, grated

50 g (2 oz) mozzarella cheese, grated

3 tablespoons freshly grated Parmesan cheese

2 tablespoons fresh white breadcrumbs

Serves 4
Preparation time: 5 minutes
Cooking time: 25 minutes

three-cheese macaroni

1 Heat the Chinese rice wine or dry sherry in a small saucepan. Add the cockles and heat through. Drain, reserving the liquid.

2 Mix 3 tablespoons of the soy sauce in a bowl with the mustard, then add the cockles.

3 Blanch the spinach briefly in lightly salted boiling water until it is just wilted. Drain thoroughly and squeeze out any excess water. Pour over the remaining soy sauce.

4 Add the reserved liquid to the cockle mixture. Arrange the spinach on a warmed serving dish, then place the cockle mixture in the centre and garnish with sesame seeds. Serve immediately.

1 tablespoon Chinese rice wine or dry sherry

250 g (8 oz) cockles, cleaned

3 tablespoons soy sauce, plus 1 teaspoon

1 teaspoon prepared strong mustard

500 g (1 lb) young spinach leaves, washed and trimmed

salt

1 tablespoon sesame seeds, to garnish

Serves 4
Preparation time: 15 minutes
Cooking time: about 10 minutes

young spinach with cockles & mustard sauce

prawn, mango & mozzarella salad
with grilled pepper salsa •
rapid-fried chilli prawns with cherry tomatoes •
griddled squid & prawns with spicy chilli sauce •
roasted scallops with cherry tomatoes •
thai fried hot fish balls •
salmon, olive & rocket baguettine •
tagliatelle with salmon cream •
griddled cod steaks with fettuccine •
red snapper with lime & coriander •
five spice fish •
sole marsala with parmesan cheese •
savoury topped fish •

speedy
fish dishes

prawn, mango & mozzarella salad with grilled pepper salsa

1 First make the grilled pepper salsa. Put the pepper on a grill rack, brush with a little oil and grill under a preheated hot grill for 10–12 minutes, turning frequently until charred all over. Transfer the pepper to a plastic bag, and set aside until cool enough to handle.

2 Skin and deseed the pepper over a bowl to catch the juices. Roughly chop the flesh and place it in a food processor or blender with the juices, the vinegar and sugar and blend until smooth. Transfer to a bowl and whisk in the oil, season with salt and pepper to taste and set aside.

3 Toss the salad leaves and radicchio with the oil in a large bowl then carefully stir in the prawns, mango and mozzarella. Divide between 4 serving plates and drizzle over the pepper salsa. Serve at once with crusty French bread.

125 g (4 oz) mixed salad leaves

25 g (1 oz) radicchio, shredded

2 tablespoons extra virgin olive oil

12 large cooked peeled prawns

1 large ripe mango, peeled, pitted and thinly sliced

150 g (5 oz) mozzarella cheese, diced

French bread, to serve

Grilled Pepper Salsa:

1 large red pepper

1 tablespoon extra virgin olive oil, plus extra for brushing

1½ teaspoons balsamic vinegar

pinch of sugar

salt and pepper

Serves 4

Preparation time: 15 minutes, plus cooling

Cooking time: 10–12 minutes

rapid-fried chilli prawns with cherry tomatoes

1 Heat a wok until hot. Add the oil and heat over a moderate heat until hot. Add the onion, ginger, garlic and chillies or chilli powder and stir-fry for 2–3 minutes, or until the onion is softened, taking care not to let the ingredients brown.

2 Add the prawns, increase the heat to high and stir-fry for 1–2 minutes, or until they turn pink. Add the tomatoes, tomato purée, wine vinegar, sugar and salt. Increase the heat to high and stir-fry for several minutes, or until the mixture is thick, taking care not to let the cherry tomatoes lose their shape. Taste and add more salt if necessary. Transfer to a warm dish and serve immediately, garnished with coriander sprigs.

3 tablespoons vegetable oil

1 small onion, finely chopped

2.5 cm (1 inch) piece of fresh root ginger, finely chopped

2 garlic cloves, crushed

1–2 fresh chillies or 1–2 tablespoons chilli powder, according to taste

375 g (12 oz) raw king or tiger prawns, peeled

6–8 cherry tomatoes, halved

2 tablespoons tomato purée

1 tablespoon red or white wine vinegar

pinch of caster sugar

½ teaspoon salt

coriander sprigs, to garnish

Serves 4 as part of an oriental meal

Preparation time: 10–15 minutes

Cooking time: 12 minutes

■ Raw king and tiger prawns are available at good fishmongers and the fresh fish counters of large supermarkets. They are expensive, but they are also large, juicy, and full of flavour – far superior to the small pale pink cooked variety. Serve this dish as part of an oriental meal, with noodles or rice.

griddled squid & prawns with spicy chilli sauce

1 To make the sauce, first heat a griddle pan. Slice the bottom off the peppers, then slice down the sides cutting them into 4–5 flat pieces, leaving the seeds on the core. Slice the chillies into wide, flat pieces, discarding the seeds. Place the pieces of pepper, skin side down, on the griddle pan and cook until the skins are charred and blistered. Cook the chillies in the same way. Place the peppers and chillies in a small dish, cover with clingfilm and leave to cool.

2 Skin the peppers and chillies and place them in a food processor, together with the sherry vinegar. Purée until smooth, then season to taste with salt and pepper. Pour the sauce into a small pan.

3 Cut the squid in half, then score in a criss-cross pattern with a sharp knife. Heat the griddle pan and cook the prawns for 2 minutes on each side. Remove and then cook the squid for 1–2 minutes on each side. They will curl up, so use a palette knife to hold them flat. Once they are cooked, cut each piece in half.

4 Add the oregano, oil, shallots and lemon juice to the chilli sauce and heat through. Toss the prawns and squid in the warm chilli sauce and serve immediately with fresh pasta.

375 g (12 oz) prepared squid, opened out

12 raw king or tiger prawns, peeled

fresh pasta, to serve

Chilli Sauce:

2 red peppers

2 fresh red chillies

2 tablespoons sherry vinegar

3 tablespoons chopped oregano

5 tablespoons olive oil

2 shallots, finely chopped

juice of ½ lemon

sea salt flakes and pepper

Serves 4

Preparation time: 20 minutes, plus cooling

Cooking time: about 10 minutes

roasted scallops
with cherry tomatoes

1 Arrange the scallops and tomato halves in a small roasting dish to fit closely together. Combine all the remaining ingredients and pour the mixture over the scallops.

2 Place the dish in a preheated oven, 230°C (450°F), Gas Mark 8, and roast for 8–10 minutes, until the scallops are just cooked. Serve immediately, garnished with the chopped parsley and lemon wedges.

■ Scallops need only a short burst in a very hot oven so that they are just cooked through. They become tough and chewy if they are over-cooked.

12 large scallops, washed and dried

12 cherry tomatoes, halved

2 garlic cloves, chopped

2 teaspoons grated lemon rind

1 tablespoon lemon juice

pinch of crushed chilli flakes

1 teaspoon chopped thyme

1 teaspoon chopped rosemary

4 tablespoons olive oil

salt and pepper

To Garnish (optional):

1 tablespoon chopped parsley

lemon wedges

Serves 2
Preparation time: 10 minutes
Cooking time: 8–10 minutes

thai fried hot fish balls

1 Put the garlic, peppercorns, coriander, sugar and dried chillies into a food processor or blender and work to a smooth paste. Add the fish fillets, a few at a time, and continue working to a smooth paste. Add the flour and soy sauce and process for a few seconds to mix. Transfer the mixture to a bowl.

2 Shape the mixture into 20 small balls, about 2.5 cm (1 inch) in diameter. Heat the oil in a wok or deep frying pan, then fry the fish balls, a few at a time, until golden brown all over. Remove with a slotted spoon, drain on kitchen paper and keep warm.

3 Arrange the cucumber slices in a serving dish. Mix together the vinegar, water, sugar, spring onions and carrot and sprinkle the mixture over the cucumber. Serve the cucumber salad with the fried hot fish balls, garnished with coriander sprigs and lime wedges.

■ Chillies vary in 'hotness' according to their variety, but whatever their type, it is the seeds that are the hottest part. Discard them if you prefer a milder chilli flavour.

4 garlic cloves, chopped

20 black peppercorns

4 coriander stems, finely chopped

pinch of sugar

3 large dried red chillies

750 g (1½ lb) fish fillets, skinned

1 tablespoon plain flour

1 tablespoon soy sauce

5 tablespoons vegetable oil

Salad:

½ cucumber, peeled and thinly sliced

1 teaspoon distilled vinegar

2 tablespoons water

1 teaspoon sugar

2 spring onions, finely chopped

1 small carrot, grated

To Garnish:

coriander sprigs

lime wedges

Serves 4
Preparation time: 15 minutes
Cooking time: 5–10 minutes

salmon, olive & rocket baguettine

1 Melt half of the butter in a heavy-based frying pan and fry the onion, sugar, salt and thyme for 15 minutes, stirring occasionally, until golden and caramelized. Set aside.

2 Slice each piece of salmon into 5 mm (¼ inch) thick slices, cutting through at a slight angle, and dust lightly with the seasoned flour.

3 Melt the remaining butter together with the oil in a nonstick frying pan and, as soon as the butter stops foaming, add the salmon strips and fry for 1 minute on each side, until golden and crispy. Remove the pan from the heat and pour in the lemon juice, stirring well.

4 Slice almost through each baguettine roll and spread with tapenade. Fill each one with rocket leaves, caramelized onion and salmon pieces and pour over the pan juices. Serve immediately.

40 g (1½ oz) butter

1 large red onion, thinly sliced

pinch of sugar

pinch of salt

1 teaspoon chopped thyme

2 x 250 g (8 oz) salmon fillets, skinned

2 tablespoons seasoned flour

2 tablespoons olive oil

juice of 1 lemon

4 baguettine rolls

4 tablespoons Tapenade (see page 9)

125 g (4 oz) rocket leaves

Serves 4
Preparation time: 10 minutes
Cooking time: 20 minutes

■ This is a fish version of a steak and onion baguette and just as tasty. A baguettine roll is the name used for a medium-sized French stick.

tagliatelle with salmon cream

1 Bring at least 1.8 litres (3 pints) water to the boil in a large saucepan. Add a dash of oil and a generous pinch of salt. Cook the pasta for 8–12 minutes, or according to the packet instructions, until just tender.

2 Meanwhile, melt the butter in a frying pan. Add the garlic and onion and fry for about 3–5 minutes, until softened but not browned. Stir in the mushrooms and fry for 4 minutes, or until they have softened. Reduce the heat and add the salmon pieces. Cook for a further 4 minutes, or until the fish is beginning to flake. Stir in the herbs and cream.

3 Drain the pasta and transfer it to a warmed serving dish. Add the sauce, stirring carefully until well mixed. Garnish with flat leaf parsley. Serve immediately with French bread and a crisp green salad, if liked.

dash of oil

425 g (14 oz) dried tagliatelle

25 g (1 oz) butter

1 garlic clove, crushed

1 onion, chopped

250 g (8 oz) assorted mushrooms, sliced if large

250 g (8 oz) salmon fillet, cubed

2 tablespoons snipped chives

1 tablespoon chopped flat leaf parsley

150 ml (¼ pint) double cream

salt

flat leaf parsley, to garnish

To Serve (optional):

French bread

green salad

Serves 4
Preparation time: 15 minutes
Cooking time: 12–15 minutes

griddled cod steaks with fettuccine

1 Heat a griddle pan or nonstick frying pan. Brush the cod steaks with a little oil and drizzle with a little lime juice and soy sauce.

2 Cook the fish on the griddle or in a frying pan for about 8 minutes on each side, or until cooked through.

3 Meanwhile, bring at least 1.8 litres (3 pints) water to the boil in a large saucepan. Add a dash of olive oil and a pinch of salt. Add the fettuccine and cook for 8–12 minutes, until just tender.

4 Drain the fettuccine and return it to the clean pan. Add the chopped parsley and stir, then drizzle with a little more olive oil, if liked. Season with salt and pepper and toss well. Spoon the fettuccine on to warmed plates and serve with the griddled fish. Garnish with wedges of lemon and lime, and parsley sprigs.

4 cod steaks, each about 150 g (5 oz)

4 tablespoons olive oil

1 teaspoon lime juice

1 teaspoon soy sauce

300 g (10 oz) dried fettuccine

2 tablespoons chopped flat leaf parsley

salt and pepper

To Garnish:

lemon wedges

lime wedges

flat leaf parsley sprigs

Serves 4
Preparation time: 10 minutes
Cooking time: 16 minutes

1 Rinse the fish fillets under cold running water and pat dry with kitchen paper. Rub the fish with half of the lime or lemon juice and 1 teaspoon of the salt and place, skin side down, in a lightly oiled, heavy-based frying pan. Add just enough cold water to cover the fish and simmer gently over a low heat for 5 minutes, turning twice.

2 Heat half the oil in another pan and add the breadcrumbs, garlic, the remaining salt and 4 tablespoons of the coriander. Cook over a low heat, stirring constantly, until the crumbs are golden brown. Spread over the fish and simmer for 7–10 minutes, until the fish flakes easily.

3 Blend the remaining lime or lemon juice and oil and pour over the fish. Cook for 2–3 minutes. Mix the remaining coriander with the lime or lemon rind and sprinkle over the fish. Season with pepper. Garnish with lime wedges and serve with warm tortillas for an authentic Mexican touch.

1 kg (2 lb) red snapper or other firm white fish, skinned and filleted

4 tablespoons lime or lemon juice

2 teaspoons salt

4 tablespoons olive oil

25 g (1 oz) fresh breadcrumbs

1 garlic clove, crushed

6 tablespoons finely chopped coriander leaves

1 teaspoon grated lime or lemon rind

pepper

lime wedges, to garnish

warm tortillas, to serve (optional)

Serves 4

Preparation time: 10 minutes

Cooking time: 20 minutes

---

red snapper with lime & coriander

five spice fish

1 Open out the mackerel and press them flat, then rinse them and dry on kitchen paper. To bone the mackerel, lay them flat on a board with the skin side upwards. Press down firmly along the length of the backbone, then turn the fish over and lift off the bones that should be freed from the flesh. Remove any small stray bones with tweezers.

2 Mix the flour with the Chinese five spice powder and sprinkle over the flesh of the mackerel. Heat a wok, then heat the vegetable oil and add the fish, arranging them so that they all fit neatly around the sides. Cook until they are brown and crisp underneath, turning them round once to ensure that they cook evenly. Then turn the fish over and cook the other side until brown and crisp.

3 Transfer the cooked fish to 4 warmed serving plates. Add the celery and lemon rind to the oil remaining in the wok and stir-fry for 2 minutes, then stir in the soy sauce. Top the fish with this mixture and garnish with spring onions and lime wedges. Serve immediately with boiled rice and a mixed salad.

4 small mackerel, gutted and heads removed

1 tablespoon plain flour

½ teaspoon Chinese five spice powder

2 tablespoons vegetable oil

1 celery stick, chopped

pared rind of 1 small lemon, finely sliced

1 tablespoon soy sauce

To Garnish:

a few spring onions, sliced

lime wedges

To Serve:

boiled rice

mixed salad leaves

Serves 4
Preparation time: 15 minutes
Cooking time: 10–15 minutes

1 Sprinkle some flour in a shallow dish and season with salt and pepper. Dip the sole into the seasoned flour to dust them lightly on both sides, then shake off any excess flour.

2 Heat the butter in a large frying pan. Add the sole and cook over a gentle heat until they are golden brown on both sides, turning them once. Sprinkle the grated Parmesan over the sole and cook them very gently for another 2–3 minutes, until the cheese melts.

3 Add the fish stock and Marsala or dry white wine. Cover the pan and cook over a very low heat for 4–5 minutes, until the sole are cooked and tender and the sauce reduced. Serve immediately sprinkled with grated Parmesan and garnished with parsley sprigs and lemon wedges.

flour, for dusting

4 Dover or lemon sole, skinned

75 g (3 oz) butter

25 g (1 oz) freshly grated Parmesan cheese, plus extra to serve

50 ml (2 fl oz) fish stock

3 tablespoons Marsala or dry white wine

salt and pepper

To Garnish:

flat leaf parsley

lemon wedges

Serves 4

Preparation time: 5 minutes

Cooking time: 12 minutes

sole marsala with parmesan cheese

savoury topped fish

1 Place the fish in a greased, shallow ovenproof dish. Spoon over the lemon juice and sprinkle with salt and pepper.

2 Melt the butter in a saucepan, add the onion and green pepper and fry until soft. Stir in the tomatoes, half of the parsley, the breadcrumbs, Cheddar and salt and pepper to taste, then spoon the mixture over the fish. Cover tightly with foil and cook in a preheated oven, 180°C (350°F), Gas Mark 4, for 30 minutes, or until the fish is tender. Sprinkle with the remaining parsley to serve.

4 cod steaks

2 tablespoons lemon juice

25 g (1 oz) butter

1 onion, finely chopped

1 green pepper, cored, deseeded and chopped

3 tomatoes, skinned and chopped

1 tablespoon chopped parsley

50 g (2 oz) fresh white breadcrumbs

75 g (3 oz) Cheddar cheese, grated

salt and pepper

Serves 4
Preparation time: 10 minutes
Cooking time: 30 minutes

griddled chicken with peanut sauce ●

green chilli chicken with spinach tagliarini ●

grilled chicken & prawn skewers ●

minced chicken with basil ●

fried chicken with peppers & onion ●

chicken in mushroom sauce ●

chicken livers oporto ●

thai duck salad ●

turkey in sweet & sour sauce ●

chicken & more

griddled chicken with peanut sauce

1 Heat a griddle pan. Add the chicken pieces and cook for 6–8 minutes on each side, or until the juices run clear when the thickest part is pierced with a knife.

2 Meanwhile, make the peanut sauce. Put the soy sauce, peanut butter, lemon juice and water into a small saucepan and season with pepper to taste. Mix well and heat gently, adjusting the consistency with a little more water if necessary.

3 When the chicken is cooked, serve with the peanut sauce drizzled over the top.

4 boneless chicken breasts or 8 boneless thighs

Peanut Sauce:

1 tablespoon soy sauce

2 tablespoons peanut butter, chunky or smooth

4 tablespoons lemon juice

4 tablespoons water

pepper

Serves 4
Preparation time: 5 minutes
Cooking time: 20 minutes

green chilli chicken with spinach tagliarini

1 Cut each chicken breast into 4 pieces. Heat a wok, then add the oil. When the oil is hot, add the chicken pieces, chillies and sliced green pepper and stir-fry for about 5 minutes, or until the chicken has browned. Stir in the lime juice, tomatoes and olives, with salt and pepper to taste. Reduce the heat and simmer the sauce for 15 minutes.

2 Meanwhile, bring at least 1.8 litres (3 pints) water to the boil in a large saucepan. Add a dash of oil and a generous pinch of salt. Add the tagliarini and cook for about 8–12 minutes, or according to packet instructions, until just tender.

3 Drain the tagliarini thoroughly. Pile it on to a large warmed serving platter and spoon the chicken mixture over it. Garnish with flat leaf parsley and serve immediately.

4 boneless, skinless chicken breasts, each about 125 g (4 oz)

1 tablespoon olive oil

2 green chillies, deseeded and sliced

1 green pepper, cored, deseeded and sliced

1 teaspoon lime juice

400 g (13 oz) can chopped Italian tomatoes

50 g (2 oz) pitted black olives

50 g (2 oz) pitted green olives

250 g (8 oz) dried spinach tagliarini

salt and pepper

flat leaf parsley, to garnish

Serves 4
Preparation time: 10 minutes
Cooking time: 20 minutes

grilled chicken & prawn skewers

1 To make the sauce, mix all the ingredients together in a bowl with salt and pepper to taste, or place in a screw-top jar and shake well.

2 Thread the pieces of chicken, prawns and peppers alternately on to pre-soaked bamboo skewers or oiled metal skewers. Place the skewers in a shallow dish and pour the sauce over them. Turn the skewers to coat thoroughly.

3 Remove the kebabs from the sauce, reserving the remainder. Cook the kebabs under a preheated hot grill for 20 minutes, turning and basting frequently with the reserved sauce. Serve hot.

750 g (1½ lb) boneless, skinless chicken breasts, cut into 2.5 cm (1 inch) cubes

20 cooked Mediterranean or large prawns, defrosted if frozen

1 small red or yellow pepper, cored, deseeded and cut into 2.5 cm (1 inch) cubes

1 small green pepper, cored, deseeded and cut into 2.5 cm (1 inch) cubes

Herb Basting Sauce:

4 tablespoons sunflower oil

2 tablespoons lemon juice

1 teaspoon chopped marjoram

1 teaspoon chopped thyme

2 tablespoons chopped flat leaf parsley

1 garlic clove, crushed

1 onion, finely chopped

salt and pepper

Serves 6–8

Preparation time: 5–10 minutes

Cooking time: 20 minutes

minced chicken with basil

1 First make the crispy garlic, shallots and basil garnish. Heat the oil in a wok. When hot, add the garlic and stir for about 40 seconds.

2 Remove with a slotted spoon, draining as much oil as possible back into the wok, then spread out to dry on absorbent kitchen paper. Repeat the process with the shallots allowing 1½–2 minutes frying time. Then add the basil and chilli to the oil and fry for about 1 minute. Remove with a slotted spoon and drain as before. Set aside.

3 To make the chicken mixture, put the chillies and garlic into a mortar and pound with a pestle until well broken down.

4 Heat the oil in a wok, add the chillies and garlic and stir-fry for 30 seconds. Add the remaining ingredients and cook, stirring, for 4 minutes over a moderate heat. Turn the heat up high and continue stirring vigorously for 30 seconds.

5 Turn on to a dish, garnish with the crispy garlic, shallots and basil mixture and serve with rice.

5 small green chillies

2 garlic cloves

2 tablespoons oil

125 g (4 oz) minced chicken

1 shallot, chopped

25 g (1 oz) bamboo shoots

25 g (1 oz) red pepper, cored, deseeded and chopped

15 g (½ oz) carrot, diced

1 teaspoon palm sugar or light muscovado sugar

3 tablespoons Thai fish sauce (nam pla) or light soy sauce

3 tablespoons chicken stock

15 g (½ oz) basil leaves, finely chopped

boiled rice, to serve

Crispy Garlic, Shallots & Basil:

25 g (1 oz) garlic, finely chopped

25 g (1 oz) shallots, finely chopped

25 g (1 oz) basil leaves

1 small red chilli, finely sliced

groundnut oil, for deep-frying

Serves 2 as a main course or 4 as a starter

Preparation time: 11 minutes

Cooking time: 11–12 minutes

fried chicken with peppers & onion

1 Sprinkle the seasoned flour on a plate. Dip the chicken joints in the flour to coat thoroughly, then shake off any excess flour.

2 Melt the butter in a heavy-based frying pan, add the chicken joints, skin side down, and fry quickly until browned. Lower the heat, arrange the joints, skin side down again – the thickest fleshy part of the joint needs most cooking – and fry gently for 25 minutes, adding the onion and pepper halfway through cooking and season with salt and pepper. Turn the joints occasionally so they cook evenly. If you like, cover the pan with a lid to keep them moist, but remove it for the last 10 minutes to allow them to crisp and brown.

3 Serve the chicken with the juices from the pan and garnish with parsley, if liked.

seasoned flour

4 chicken joints

50–75 g (2–3 oz) butter

1 large onion, sliced

1 green pepper, cored, deseeded and finely sliced

salt and pepper

parsley sprigs, to garnish (optional)

Serves 4
Preparation time: 5–10 minutes
Cooking time: 30 minutes

■ As a spicy variation, add 1 teaspoon curry powder to every 2 tablespoons flour and use for coating the chicken before frying.

chicken in mushroom sauce

1 Dust the chicken with the cornflour until thoroughly coated. Shake off any excess. Heat the oil and gently fry the chicken breasts for about 5 minutes on each side, or until cooked through. Drain well on kitchen paper and keep warm.

2 To make the sauce, melt the butter and stir-fry the shallot and mushrooms for 1 minute. Put the cream, water, mustard, soy sauce and cornflour into a small bowl and mix until smooth, then add to the mushroom mixture and cook, stirring, until the mixture has thickened. Season with salt and pepper. Spoon the sauce over the chicken and serve garnished with watercress.

■ Do not let the sauce boil after you have added the cream or it may curdle.

6 boneless, skinless chicken breasts, each about 125 g (4 oz)

25 g (1 oz) cornflour, sifted

2 tablespoons oil

watercress sprigs, to garnish

Mushroom Sauce:

25 g (1 oz) butter, softened

1 shallot, finely chopped

175 g (6 oz) mushrooms, finely chopped

5 tablespoons single cream

5 tablespoons cold water

¼ teaspoon Dijon mustard

1 teaspoon soy sauce

1 teaspoon cornflour

salt and pepper

Serves 6
Preparation time: 5 minutes
Cooking time: 15 minutes

1 Heat the butter and oil in a large, heavy-based frying pan, add the livers and celery and sauté gently for 3–4 minutes, until the livers are golden outside but still pink inside. When cooked, remove the livers from the pan and keep warm.

2 To make the sauce, add the port to the pan and simmer for a few minutes, until slightly reduced. Add the soured cream, tilting the pan to mix, and continue cooking gently until a smooth sauce forms. Season to taste with salt and pepper.

3 Spoon the sauce equally on to 4 individual serving plates and serve the livers on top of it, garnished with celery leaves. Pasta tossed in garlic-flavoured butter would make a good accompaniment.

25g (1 oz) butter

1 tablespoon oil

500 g (1 lb) chicken livers, trimmed and halved

3 celery sticks, sliced

4 tablespoons port

5 tablespoons soured cream

salt and pepper

celery leaves, to garnish

pasta tossed in garlic-flavoured butter, to serve (optional)

Serves 4
Preparation time: 10 minutes
Cooking time: 10 minutes

chicken livers oporto

▓ Don't let the chicken livers over-cook or they will become hard and lose their delicious soft, melting texture.

¼ ready-cooked roast duck

6 small green chillies, thinly sliced

½ red onion, thinly sliced

25 g (1 oz) coriander leaves, stalks and roots, finely chopped

½ tomato, cut into quarters

juice of 2 limes

1 heaped teaspoon palm sugar or light muscovado sugar

4½ teaspoons Thai fish sauce

To Serve:

lettuce leaves

mint leaves

1 Remove all the skin and meat from the duck and cut them into bite-size pieces.

2 Heat a wok, then turn the heat off. Put the duck into the wok to warm it through and then add all the remaining ingredients, stirring and turning them thoroughly for 3 minutes.

3 To serve, arrange the lettuce leaves and mint on one side of a serving dish and place the warm duck salad beside them.

Serves 2
Preparation time: 8–10 minutes

thai duck salad

turkey in sweet & sour sauce

1 Toss the turkey strips in the cornflour. Heat a wok, then heat the oil and fry the turkey strips over a moderately high heat for 3 minutes, stirring occasionally. Remove the meat and drain it on kitchen paper.

2 To make the sauce, put the cornflour into a measuring jug. Gradually stir in the water to make a smooth paste, then stir in all the remaining sauce ingredients. Pour the sauce into the wok and bring to the boil, stirring. Simmer for 1 minute, still stirring, then add the turkey and simmer for 5 minutes over a low heat.

3 Heat the butter in a small saucepan, add the mushrooms and fry over a moderate heat for 2 minutes, then stir them into the sauce. Serve with boiled rice.

4 turkey breast portions, total weight about 500 g (1 lb), cut into 5 x 1 cm (2 x ½ inch) strips

2 teaspoons cornflour

2 tablespoons vegetable oil

15 g (½ oz) butter

125 g (4 oz) mushrooms, thinly sliced

boiled rice, to serve

Sweet & Sour Sauce:

1½ teaspoons cornflour

4–6 tablespoons water

4½ teaspoons soft light brown sugar

4½ teaspoons clear honey

3 tablespoons red wine vinegar

3 tablespoons tomato purée

3 tablespoons orange juice

3 tablespoons soy sauce

salt

Serves 4
Preparation time: 10–15 minutes
Cooking time: 15 minutes

quick meat dinners

mangetout & beef stir-fry

1 Combine the ginger, garlic, soy sauce, sherry, chilli sauce, honey and five spice powder in a non-metallic bowl and stir well. Add the beef, stir to coat thoroughly, then leave to marinate until required.

2 Bring at least 1.8 litres (3 pints) water to the boil in a large saucepan. Add a dash of oil and a pinch of salt. Add the noodles, then remove the pan from the heat, cover and leave to stand for 5 minutes.

3 Meanwhile, heat a wok, then add the sesame oil. When the oil is hot, transfer the meat to the wok with a slotted spoon and stir-fry for about 3 minutes. Add the mangetout and the marinade, season with salt and pepper if required, and stir-fry over a medium heat for a further 2 minutes.

4 Drain the noodles and arrange them on a platter. Spoon the stir-fry over the top and garnish with shredded spring onions.

25 g (1 oz) piece of fresh root ginger, shredded

1 garlic clove, crushed

4 tablespoons soy sauce

2 tablespoons dry sherry

1 teaspoon chilli sauce

1 teaspoon clear honey

½ teaspoon Chinese five spice powder

500 g (1 lb) fillet steak, thinly sliced

1 tablespoon sesame oil

250 g (8 oz) dried egg noodles

250 g (8 oz) mangetout, trimmed

salt and pepper

spring onions, shredded, to garnish

Serves 4

Preparation time: 10 minutes

Cooking time: about 10 minutes

◼ Five spice powder is a piquant Chinese condiment, made from a mixture of ground spices: star anise, fennel seeds, cloves, cinnamon and Sichuan pepper.

beef stroganoff

1 Heat half the butter in a sauté pan and fry the onions until soft. Add the mushrooms and pepper to the pan and cook for 5 minutes. Remove the onions, mushrooms and pepper from the pan.

2 Heat the remaining butter, then fry the meat for about 4 minutes, turning it so it becomes evenly cooked on all sides.

3 Return the onions, mushrooms and pepper to the pan, season well, stir in the crème fraîche or soured cream and blend well. Heat until pining hot but do not allow to boil. Garnish with chopped parsley, if liked, and serve immediately.

50 g (2 oz) butter

3 onions, finely chopped

250 g (8 oz) mushrooms, thinly sliced

1 green pepper, cored, deseeded and cut into fine strips

500 g (1 lb) fillet or good rump steak, cut into strips 5 cm (2 inches) long, 5 mm (¼ inch) thick

150 ml (¼ pint) crème fraîche or soured cream

salt and pepper

1 tablespoon chopped parsley, to garnish (optional)

Serves 4

Preparation time: 10 minutes

Cooking time: 15 minutes

■ To make a more economic version of this dish, use a cheaper cut of meat such as braising steak. Cut the meat into thin strips and marinate them overnight in lemon juice to tenderize them.

green peppercorn steak

1 Preheat a griddle pan until it is very hot. Cook the steaks for 2–3 minutes on each side, then remove them from the pan, set aside and keep warm.

2 Add the green peppercorns, soy sauce, balsamic vinegar and cherry tomatoes to the griddle pan. Allow the liquids to sizzle for about 2 minutes, or until the tomatoes are soft. Spoon the sauce over the steaks and garnish with thyme. Serve with potatoes, if liked.

■ Green peppercorns are the unripe fruit of *Piper nigrum*, black pepper, and have a much milder flavour.

4 lean fillet steaks, each about 75 g (3 oz)

1 tablespoon green peppercorns in brine, drained

2 tablespoons light soy sauce

1 teaspoon balsamic vinegar

8 cherry tomatoes, halved

thyme sprigs, to garnish

potatoes, to serve (optional)

Serves 4
Preparation time: 5 minutes
Cooking time: 6–8 minutes

1 Blanch the okra in lightly salted boiling water for 5 minutes, then drain, rinse under cold running water and drain again. Set aside.

2 Heat a wok, then heat the vegetable oil over a moderate heat. Add the onion, garlic, coriander, turmeric and chilli powder and stir-fry for 2–3 minutes, or until the onion is softened, taking care not to let the onion brown. Add the lamb strips to the wok, increase the heat to high and stir-fry for 3–4 minutes, or until the lamb is browned all over.

3 Add the tomatoes and stir-fry until the juices run, then add the lemon rind and juice, sugar and salt to taste. Stir-fry to mix, then add the okra and toss for 3–4 minutes, or until heated through. Serve hot.

250 g (8 oz) small okra, trimmed

3 tablespoons vegetable oil

1 onion, thinly sliced

1–2 garlic cloves, crushed

2 teaspoons ground coriander

2 teaspoons ground turmeric

1 teaspoon hot chilli powder, or to taste

500 g (1 lb) lamb fillet, cut into thin strips across the grain

250 g (8 oz) ripe tomatoes, skinned and roughly chopped

finely grated rind and juice of ½ lemon

½ teaspoon caster sugar

salt

Serves 3–4
Preparation time: 15 minutes
Cooking time: about 18 minutes

lamb with okra & tomatoes

lamb in lettuce parcels

1 First make the dipping sauce. Beat together all the ingredients in a small bowl. Set aside.

2 Heat a wok, then heat the oil in the wok over a moderate heat until hot. Add the spring onions, chilli and garlic and stir-fry for 2–3 minutes to flavour the oil. Remove all the flavourings with a slotted spoon and drain on kitchen paper.

3 Drain the mushrooms, squeeze dry and chop roughly. Add the lamb to the wok and increase the heat to high. Stir-fry for 3–4 minutes, or until browned all over. Add the mushrooms and bean sprouts and stir-fry for 2–3 minutes, then return the spring onion mixture to the wok and add the soy sauce. Stir-fry until all the ingredients are evenly combined, then add pepper to taste.

4 Spoon a little hoisin sauce on to each lettuce leaf, place a few mint or basil leaves on top, then a spoonful of the lamb mixture. Roll up the lettuce around the lamb tucking the ends in. Serve immediately, with the dipping sauce handed separately.

2 tablespoons vegetable oil

½ bunch of spring onions, thinly sliced on the diagonal

1 green chilli, deseeded and finely chopped

2 garlic cloves, crushed

15 g (½ oz) dried shiitake mushrooms, soaked in warm water for 20 minutes

250 g (8 oz) lamb fillet, cut into thin strips across the grain

75 g (3 oz) bean sprouts

3 tablespoons soy sauce

about 4 tablespoons hoisin sauce

8 crisp lettuce leaves

mint or basil leaves

pepper

Dipping Sauce:

125 ml (4 fl oz) soy sauce

2 garlic cloves, crushed

1 teaspoon caster sugar

1 teaspoon lemon juice

Serves 4

Preparation time: 15 minutes

Cooking time: about 12 minutes

sausage frittata

1 Heat the vegetable oil in a frying pan, add the onion and fry gently for about 8 minutes, until soft and lightly golden. Add the potatoes and fry until they are just beginning to colour, turning them frequently but lightly. Add the sausage and stir-fry for 1 minute, then stir in the peas.

2 Beat the eggs in a bowl with salt and pepper to taste. Pour the mixture into the frying pan, reduce the heat and leave the frittata to cook, without stirring, until the egg is just beginning to set at the edges.

3 Sprinkle the top of the frittata with the grated cheese and paprika. Slide the frying pan under a preheated hot grill and leave until the top of the frittata is golden and bubbly. Carefully ease the egg away from the sides of the pan and slide the frittata on to a serving dish. Cut into wedges and serve hot or cold, accompanied by mixed salad leaves.

6 tablespoons vegetable oil

2 small onions, sliced

2 potatoes, boiled and diced

250 g (8 oz) Dutch smoked sausage, sliced

175 g (6 oz) frozen peas

6 eggs, lightly beaten

125 g (4 oz) Cheddar cheese, grated

paprika, to taste

salt and pepper

mixed salad leaves, to serve

Serves 4–6
Preparation time: 10 minutes
Cooking time: 20 minutes

■ A frittata is an Italian version of the omelette, but in this case the eggs are cooked for at least 10 minutes over a low heat, with the vegetables or other ingredients cooked in the egg mixture. A frittata is served flat rather than folded.

fried pork with baby corn

1 Mix the Chinese rice wine or dry sherry and soy sauce with 1 teaspoon of the cornflour. Add the pork and toss to coat well.

2 Heat a wok, then heat the sunflower oil and stir-fry the pork until it is lightly browned. Add the baby corn cobs and salt and stir-fry for 30 seconds. Add the mangetout and mushrooms and stir-fry for 1 minute. Sprinkle in the sugar.

3 Mix the remaining cornflour with the water to make a smooth thin paste and add this to the wok. Cook, stirring constantly, until the sauce is thickened. Transfer to a warmed serving dish and serve immediately.

1 tablespoon Chinese rice wine or dry sherry

1 tablespoon light soy sauce

1½ teaspoons cornflour

500 g (1 lb) pork fillet, sliced as thinly as possible

1 tablespoon sunflower oil

500 g (1 lb) baby corn cobs

1 teaspoon salt

50 g (2 oz) mangetout

425 g (14 oz) can straw mushrooms, drained

2 teaspoons sugar

2 teaspoons water

Serves 4

Preparation time: 5 minutes

Cooking time: about 5 minutes

pork with chilli & basil

1 Heat a wok, then heat the oil. Add the garlic and chillies and stir-fry until the garlic is just golden. Add the pork, pepper, fish sauce and sugar, stirring constantly.

2 Stir in the bamboo shoots, if using, with the onion, red pepper and stock. Cook for 5 minutes. Stir in the basil leaves and cook for 1 minute more. Garnish with basil leaves and large slices of red chilli. Serve at once with boiled rice.

◼ As a variation, stir-fry the garlic and chillies as in the main recipe, then substitute 125 g (4 oz) rump steak for the pork and continue as above.

2 tablespoons vegetable oil

1 garlic clove, crushed

2 chillies, finely chopped, or to taste

125 g (4 oz) pork fillet, thinly sliced

¼ teaspoon pepper

1 tablespoon Thai fish sauce

½ teaspoon sugar

50 g (2 oz) canned bamboo shoots, very finely sliced (optional)

2 tablespoons finely chopped onion

2 tablespoons thinly sliced red pepper

4 tablespoons chicken or vegetable stock

2 handfuls of basil, plus extra to garnish

3–4 large red chillies, sliced, to garnish

boiled rice, to serve

Serves 4 as part of an oriental meal

Preparation time: 10 minutes

Cooking time: 10–12 minutes

creamed veal

1 Melt the butter with the oil in a large frying pan, add the veal and fry quickly to seal and brown on all sides. Using a slotted spoon, remove the veal from the pan and set aside.

2 Add the onions to the fat remaining in the pan and fry gently for about 10 minutes, until soft and golden. Add the mushrooms and cook for 2–3 minutes more.

3 Return the veal to the pan, season to taste with salt and pepper and cook gently for a further 2–3 minutes, or until the veal is tender and cooked through.

4 Stir in the double cream, chopped parsley and mint and reheat gently. Transfer to a warmed serving dish, garnish with the mint sprigs and serve immediately.

25 g (1 oz) butter

2 tablespoons corn oil

500–750 g (1–1½ lb) lean veal fillet, thinly sliced

2 onions, finely chopped

250 g (8 oz) mushrooms, sliced

150 ml (¼ pint) double cream

4 tablespoons chopped parsley

4 teaspoons chopped mint

salt and pepper

mint sprigs, to garnish

Serves 4
Preparation time: 10 minutes
Cooking time: about 20 minutes

1 Strip about 12 leaves from the tarragon, chop them roughly and reserve. Put the cream into a small saucepan with the remaining tarragon. Bring slowly to the boil then remove the pan from the heat. Cover the pan and leave for 20 minutes to infuse, stirring occasionally.

2 Melt the butter in a frying pan. When it is very hot, add the escalopes and cook quickly, 2 minutes on each side should be enough. Transfer to a plate and keep warm.

3 Pour the tarragon-flavoured cream through a sieve into the frying pan and stir well to mix with the pan juices. Add about 1 tablespoon lemon juice, or to taste, and plenty of salt and pepper and mix well. Pour the sauce over the escalopes and sprinkle with the reserved tarragon leaves. Serve with new potatoes or rice, and a crisp green salad.

6 tarragon sprigs

300 ml (½ pint) double cream

40 g (1½ oz) butter

4 veal escalopes

juice of ½ small lemon

sea salt and pepper

To Serve:

new potatoes or rice

green salad

Serves 4

Preparation time: 10 minutes, plus infusing

Cooking time: about 10 minutes

veal with tarragon

chinese banana fritters ●
strawberries with butterscotch sauce ●
apricot toasts ●
figs & blackberries on toast ●
pineapple with rumbled mascarpone ●
rhubarb fool ●
exotic ruby fruit salad ●
lemon crunch flan ●
black cherry flan ●
blackcurrant muffins ●
ginger cookies ●
no-cook chocolate nut slice ●

short & sweet

chinese banana fritters

1 Sift the flours and salt into a bowl. Add the cold water and whisk thoroughly to make a smooth, coating batter. Stir in the grated lime rind.

2 Heat a wok, then heat the oil in the wok or in a deep-fryer. Meanwhile, peel the bananas, spear them one at a time with a skewer and dip them into the batter until they are evenly coated. Deep-fry the bananas in batches until they are crisp and golden. Remove with a slotted spoon and drain on kitchen paper.

3 Transfer the fritters to a serving dish and serve hot with the lime quarters and sugar for sprinkling.

■ If possible, buy very small bananas for these fritters. They look better than large ones and are usually sweeter in flavour. You are most likely to find them in Asian grocery stores.

125 g (4 oz) self-raising flour
40 g (1½ oz) rice flour
½ teaspoon salt
200 ml (7 fl oz) cold water
finely grated rind of 1 lime
vegetable oil, for deep-frying
8 small bananas

To Serve:
1–2 limes, cut into quarters
caster sugar, to taste

Serves 8
Preparation time: 15 minutes
Cooking time: 12–15 minutes

strawberries with butterscotch sauce

1 To make the sauce, put the sugar and golden syrup into a heavy-based saucepan and cook over a low heat, stirring occasionally, until the sugar has dissolved. Cook for a further 5 minutes.

2 Remove the pan from the heat and stir in the cream and vanilla essence. Beat for about 2 minutes, until the sauce is smooth and glossy.

3 Put the strawberries into a serving bowl, and serve the sauce hot or cold.

750 g (1½ lb) fresh strawberries, hulled and halved if large

Butterscotch Sauce:

150 g (5 oz) soft light brown sugar

150 g (5 oz) golden syrup

125 ml (4 fl oz) double cream

3–4 drops vanilla essence

Serves 4
Preparation time: 15 minutes
Cooking time: 10 minutes

apricot toasts

1 Beat together the egg and milk and pour into a shallow dish. Dip the bread slices into the mixture until they are coated on both sides and have absorbed the egg mixture.

2 Melt the butter in a frying pan and fry the slices of bread until crisp and golden on both sides. Drain on kitchen paper.

3 Mix the sugar and cinnamon and sprinkle on to the bread. Top with the apricots, whipped cream and nuts and serve immediately.

■ Bread, whether sweet or plain, dipped into a custard mixture and pan-fried is known in France as *Pain Perdu* and England as Poor Knights of Windsor. The recipe dates back to medieval times.

1 egg

1 tablespoon milk

4–8 small slices fruited or plain bread, crusts removed

40 g (1½ oz) butter

2 tablespoons caster sugar

½ teaspoon ground cinnamon

300 g (10 oz) can apricot halves in juice, drained

150 ml (¼ pint) whipping cream, whipped

1 tablespoon chopped pistachios or toasted almonds

Serves 4

Preparation time: 10 minutes

Cooking time: 5 minutes

figs & blackberries on toast

1 Cut the figs into quarters, slicing almost but not all the way through, so that the quarters fall back like flower petals. Cut 4 squares of double-thickness foil and place 3 figs and a quarter of the blackberries on each piece of foil. Cut the orange rind into julienne strips. Place in a bowl, stir in the orange juice and the crème de cassis and divide among the fig parcels. Bring up the edges of the foil and press to seal. Mix the sugar, cinnamon and melted butter in a bowl and brush over one side of each brioche or bread slice.

2 Cook the fig parcels in a preheated oven, 200°C (400°F), Gas Mark 6, for about 8–10 minutes, or until the figs are hot and slightly soft. Towards the end of the cooking time, add the buttered brioche or bread slices to a preheated moderately hot griddle, buttered side up, and toast until crisp and golden.

3 Serve the cinnamon toasts on individual serving plates, topped with the figs and blackberries. Add a spoonful of fromage frais or Greek yogurt, if liked.

12 ripe figs

125 g (4 oz) blackberries

pared rind and juice of 2 oranges

2 tablespoons crème de cassis

1 tablespoon caster sugar

½ teaspoon cinnamon

25 g (1 oz) butter, melted

4 slices brioche or white bread

fromage frais or Greek yogurt, to serve (optional)

Serves 4
Preparation time: 10–15 minutes
Cooking time: 8–10 minutes

Crème de cassis is a French liqueur made from blackcurrants. As well as adding a depth of flavour to desserts such as this one, it also makes a delicious summer drink stirred into a glass of white wine.

1 pineapple, peeled, cored and sliced

6 tablespoons mascarpone cheese

2 tablespoons light rum

2 tablespoons fine brown sugar

1 Heat a griddle pan, add the pineapple slices and cook for 2 minutes on each side.

2 Mix together the mascarpone, rum and brown sugar. Serve the pineapple with the mascarpone mixture spooned over the top.

Serves 4
Preparation time: 5 minutes
Cooking time: 10 minutes

pineapple with rumbled mascarpone

rhubarb fool

1 Trim the rhubarb stalks of any leaves or brown roots. Chop the stalks into 5 cm (2 inch) lengths and put them into a heavy-based saucepan with the demerara sugar and orange rind and just a little water. Simmer for about 5 minutes, or until the rhubarb is tender.

2 Pour off the excess juice then sieve the fruit, purée it in a food processor or leave it whole.

3 When cold, lightly stir in the cream and the Pernod, if using, aiming for an attractive marbled effect. Serve the fool decorated with the stem ginger, if liked.

1 kg (2 lb) young rhubarb

125–175 g (4–6 oz) demerara sugar

finely grated rind of 1 small orange

275 ml (9 fl oz) double cream, softly whipped

2 teaspoons Pernod (optional)

a little finely chopped stem ginger in syrup, to decorate (optional)

Serves 4

Preparation time: 10 minutes, plus cooling

Cooking time: about 5 minutes

■ For a less rich dessert, serve the stewed rhubarb with some crème fraîche or thick Greek yogurt sprinkled with a little demerara sugar.

exotic ruby fruit salad

1 Prepare all the fruit according to type. Cut it into bite-size pieces and place in a serving bowl.

2 Split open the cardamom pods, take out the little black seeds and grind them finely using a pestle and mortar or a spice mill. Sprinkle the seeds over the fruit.

3 Combine the orange juice and liqueur in a jug, pour over the fruit and stir well to coat.

1.5 kg (3 lb) tropical fruits (e.g. mango, papaya, pineapple, lychee, tamarillo, guava, physalis) or other fruits of your choice

4 green cardamom pods

300 ml (½ pint) freshly squeezed ruby red orange juice

1 tablespoon Grand Marnier or Cointreau

Serves 4–6

Preparation time: 15 minutes

 The flavour of this fruit salad will be enhanced and the fruit will take on an even deeper red if it is left to macerate for about 2-3 hours before serving.

175 g (6 oz) digestive biscuits, crushed

75 g (3 oz) butter, melted

150 ml (¼ pint) double cream

215 g (7½ oz) can sweetened condensed milk

finely grated rind of 1 lemon

6 tablespoons lemon juice

To Decorate:

2 digestive biscuits, crushed

whipped cream

lemon slices, quartered

Serves 6

Preparation time: 25 minutes, plus chilling

---

1 Put the crushed biscuits in a bowl and stir in the melted butter. Mix well and press over the base of a 20 cm (8 inch) flan ring placed on a baking sheet. Place in the refrigerator to chill for 10 minutes.

2 Lightly whip the cream and stir in the condensed milk and lemon rind and juice. Whip until thoroughly blended, then pour evenly on to the prepared biscuit base and chill in the refrigerator until set.

3 Decorate the flan with biscuit crumbs, whirls of cream and quartered lemon slices.

lemon crunch flan

black cherry flan

1 Place the flan case on a large serving plate.

2 Mix the sugar, rum and water in a heavy-based saucepan. Place over a low heat and bring to the boil, stirring constantly. Boil vigorously, without stirring, for 2–3 minutes. Pour the syrup into the flan case.

3 In a bowl, beat the cheese, honey, cinnamon and cream, then spread the mixture in the flan case. Arrange the cherries over the cheese mixture. Glaze with the warmed cherry jam.

1 large ready-made sponge flan case

125 g (4 oz) sugar

3 tablespoons light rum

3 tablespoons water

250 g (8 oz) low-fat soft cheese

2 tablespoons clear honey

pinch of ground cinnamon

1 tablespoon single cream

500 g (1 lb) black cherries, pitted

3 tablespoons black cherry jam, warmed

Serves 8

Preparation time: 10–15 minutes

Cooking time: 5 minutes

blackcurrant muffins

1 Line a muffin or bun tin with paper cake cases.

2 Sift the flour, baking powder and salt into a large bowl. Stir in the sugar and blackcurrants.

3 Whisk the egg with the milk and melted butter. Stir into the dry ingredients until just mixed – do not over-mix. Spoon the mixture into the cake cases and bake in a preheated oven, 220°C (425°F), Gas Mark 7, for 15–20 minutes, until well risen and a skewer inserted into the centre comes out clean. Serve the muffins warm straight from the oven.

175 g (6 oz) plain flour

1 tablespoon baking powder

½ teaspoon salt

75 g (3 oz) caster sugar

150 g (5 oz) blackcurrants

1 egg, beaten

175 ml (6 fl oz) milk

125 g (4 oz) butter, melted and cooled

Makes 9

Preparation time: 10 minutes

Cooking time: 15–20 minutes

ginger cookies

1 Grease 2 baking sheets. Sift the flour, bicarbonate of soda, ground ginger and caster sugar into a bowl. Melt the butter with the golden syrup and stir into the sifted mixture with the chopped stem ginger.

2 With wetted hands, break off walnut-sized pieces of cookie dough and roll into balls. Place the balls slightly apart on the baking sheets and flatten lightly with a palette knife. Arrange a flaked almond on top of each one.

3 Bake the cookies in a preheated oven, 200°C (400°F), Gas Mark 6, for 8–10 minutes. Leave to cool slightly on the baking sheets then transfer to a wire rack to cool completely.

125 g (4 oz) self-raising flour

½ teaspoon bicarbonate of soda

2 teaspoons ground ginger

1 tablespoon caster sugar

50 g (2 oz) butter

75 g (3 oz) golden syrup

1 tablespoon chopped stem ginger in syrup

about 24 flaked almonds

Makes about 24

Preparation time: 20 minutes

Cooking time: 8–10 minutes

no-cook chocolate nut slice

1 Line the base and 1.5 cm (¾ inch) up the sides of an 18 cm (7 inch) square shallow baking tin or cake tin with the rice paper.

2 Put the chocolate and butter into a heatproof bowl set over a pan of barely simmering water and leave until melted.

3 Stir the biscuits and nuts into the melted chocolate, then turn the mixture into the prepared tin. Spread the mixture evenly, then chill for several hours or overnight until firm.

4 To serve, remove the cake from the tin and either cut or break it into small pieces.

edible rice paper

375 g (12 oz) plain dark chocolate, broken into pieces

175 g (6 oz) unsalted butter

125 g (4 oz) digestive biscuits, chopped into small pieces

175 g (6 oz) mixed whole nuts (almonds, hazelnuts, Brazil nuts)

Makes 14–16 slices

Preparation time: 15 minutes, plus chilling

index